This book is dedicated to all those overcoming life's challenges. You can do it!

A special dedication to Joyce, who is always with us and reminds us to never give up.

IVy
the VERY DETERMINED DOG
A TRUE STORY

By: Chris and Maureen Harrington

Illustrated by: Charlotte Bruijn

This is the story of a dog named Ivy.
She loved to run, play and was always lively!

Strong and fast, though she was small—
So much fun, and loved by all.

One cold winter's night, tired and lame,
Ivy howled—"My back is in pain!"

Her family wanted the pain to go away,
So they packed up her toys for a hospital stay.

The doctor said softly, "We need to talk,
It'll now be hard for Ivy to walk."

Ivy and her parents had tears in their eyes,
This challenging news came as quite a surprise.

Several days passed and Ivy turned glum.
"I miss my back legs and want to have fun!"

Dreaming of when she ran free,
Ivy thought, *It's up to me...*

Tips & Tricks: how to catch a ball on 2 paws

NOW WHAT?

DIFFERENT DOG

HAPPY DOG

I'm different, but that's okay,
I'm still Ivy. I love to play!

The next day, when she woke up to eat,
It happened—she could walk on two feet!

The phrase, "I can't," turned into, "I can."

"I will walk again—that is my plan!"

She grew stronger and stronger each step she took,

I know I can do it,
was her new outlook.

Ivy soon made a new friend, his name was Eddie.
"I know how you feel, I've been through this already."

"Here's a wheelchair, it's my gift to you,
Now you can run fast like you used to."

She rolled through the park with her head held high.
Her new wheels made her feel like she could fly!

Ivy was happy with what she had done,
She never gave up or stopped having fun.

Ivy the Very Determined Dog was her new name.
Although she was different, she was really the same.

Always remember when you're down in the dumps,
The story of Ivy and all her triumphs!

Just keep on rolling, whatever you do,
And never let your troubles get the better of you!

Fun Facts about Ivy

Why did Ivy lose use of her back legs?
Ivy was diagnosed at age three with a genetic spinal disease called Intervertebral Disc Disease (also known as IVDD). The deeper meaning behind her new nickname Ivy the **V**ery **D**etermined **D**og comes from IVDD.

Where is Ivy from?
Gloucester, MA. (she loves the sand between her paws)

Massachusetts
IVY
The Spirit of America

What is Ivy's favorite activity?
When she is not rolling around town, she can be found catching up on sleep. Ivy is also a big fan of belly rubs!

Who are Ivy's best friends shown in the book?
Her girlfriends Annie the black lab & Hazel the yellow lab, and her boyfriend Banx the boxer.

What is Ivy's favorite food? Cheese please!

Who is Eddie in the book?
Ivy's wheels were custom made by Eddie's Wheels in Shelburne Falls, Massachusetts. It's only fitting that her friend in the park was named Eddie.

Ivy's parents!

When is Ivy's birthday?
December 1, 2013

What is Ivy's favorite toy?
A purple unicorn... because it's magical just like her.

THANK YOU!

Thank you for your Pawsitivity throughout my journey and helping me to share my story with the world! You rock, I roll!

Copyright © 2019 by Christopher & Maureen Harrington
Illustrations by Charlotte Bruijn

Published by Bromfield Press, LLC.

All rights reserved.

No part of this publication, or the characters within it, may be reproduced or distributed in any form or by any means without the prior written consent from the publisher.

ISBN: 9781732777101
Second Edition
Printed in the USA.

A portion of proceeds of this book will be donated to various non-profit organizations. Bromfield Press provides special discounts when purchased in larger volumes for fundraising and educational use. Please contact us at bromfieldpressllc@gmail.com.

Elaine & Michael Brennan & Auntie Annie
Sharon & Marc Harrington & Mr. Banx
Elizabeth & Adam Mara & Hazel Mae
Rosie Harrington (my new adopted sister!)
Kerri & Nick Petri
Charlie Petri
Callie & Aubrey Sullivan
Dr. Gena Silver
Dr. Bronwyn Riggs
Woburn Veterinary Referral Hospital
Perfect Paws Pet Ministry
Woburn Animal Hospital
Frenchie Bulldog Pet Supply
Gia Flowers & Family
Brady Scalzo and Family
Tiffany Baker
Eddies Wheels
The Long Family
The Bennett Family
Fio Bordonaro
Amy Mara
Candace Gatti
Kathy & Peter Coakley
Kathy & Neil Harrington
Michael Anagnos
Mrs. Griffith's 4th Grade Class Harrington Elementary
Vitaly Fedosik
Ashleigh and Brendan McCourt
Monsieur Louie & Ferguson Family
Timothy & Bailey Haroutunian
Poppy the Pembroke Welsh Corgi
Eva Bannon Pouliot
Michelle Palmero
Devin Ikram & Nikita
Stella
Sigmund Russo
Ella and Coco Bishop
Mackenzie & Cheese Quick
Kathryn Hearn
Titan & Lola
Holly, Giada, Mia, Bailee, Emmersyn, Jackson
Maya Tisdale
Roman Dinkel
Regan Smith
Duke & Abi
Bethanee Hamilton
Road Dogs
Smiles Taylor
The Dodo
The Little Things
Trupanion Pet Insurance